MY DAD LOVES ME

Written and illustrated by
Melissa Lee

Archway Publishing books may be ordered through booksellers or by contacting:

Archway Publishing
1663 Liberty Drive
Bloomington, IN 47403
www.archwaypublishing.com
844-669-3957

Written and illustrated by Melissa Lee

ISBN: 978-1-6657-1175-3 (sc)
ISBN: 978-1-6657-1176-0 (hc)
ISBN: 978-1-6657-1177-7 (e)

Print information available on the last page.

Archway Publishing rev. date: 07/28/2022

My Dad
Loves Me

Dedication

For my grandson, Nicholas whose love for his father endures and for my son, Dimitri, who will always love him...

Back in the day like some people say...

Before Pre K...

Before soccer on Saturday...

Before I even knew how to play...

My dad loved me.

Back when everything was new ...

Before I even had a clue...

Before you knew me,
Before I knew you ...

My dad loved me.

Back when I was in my crib...

Before I ate without a bib...

Before I drank from a cup,
Before I could even sit up...

My dad loved me.

Back when I was only two,
Before we had the time to do,

**So many things that
dads and sons
Do together one on one...**

He was gone...

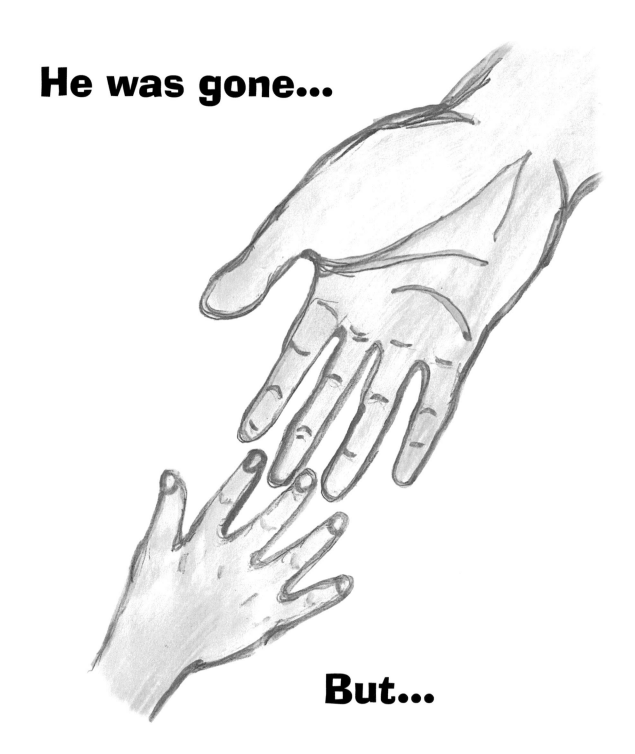

But...

My dad loved me.

Now whenever I wonder why...

Now, whenever I start to cry...

**Before I shed too many tears,
I know that after all
these years...**

My
dad
loves
me.

And he always will...

In memory of
Dimitri Grammatikopoulos

About the Author

Melissa Lee has enjoyed writing creatively since childhood. She holds a BA in psychology and an MS in elementary education. A native New Yorker, she spent twenty-seven years as an elementary school teacher, but her favorite job is being a mother and grandmother.

Printed in the United States
by Baker & Taylor Publisher Services